THE SHOW MUST GO ON!

Paul Harvey

Illustrated by **George Bletsis**

OXFORD
UNIVERSITY PRESS

Contents

Break a Leg!

Have you ever been to the theatre? Maybe you've seen a musical with your family. Perhaps you've been on a school trip to see a production of one of the many plays of William Shakespeare, England's most famous playwright. Did you ever wonder how a theatrical production starts as an idea and becomes a reality? I'll tell you how!

A musical version of Roald Dahl's *Matilda*

My name's Paul and I'm a trained actor.

I started acting at school. I had a wonderful teacher, Mr Mortimer. He really encouraged me and I liked acting so much I decided to study drama at university. After that I did lots of shows in theatres in London, but I wanted to help children enjoy acting the way I had when I was at school, so I became a teacher of English and Drama.

I have worked with thousands of students all over the world to put on shows in Sudan, Egypt, Turkey, Morocco and the United Kingdom (UK). I have also appeared in theatres in Oxford and in some open-air Shakespeare productions too.

One of the best things about being in a show is that feeling of nervous excitement just before you go on stage – sometimes in front of a lot of people!

I'm going to share my backstage secrets to putting on a show with you. You'll learn about all the different people who come together to make the production happen, and the decisions you need to make when you're putting on a show. I'll take you behind the scenes of the professional world of theatre to explain everything from how to create monstrous make-up to how to fight safely. Once you know all that, you might be able to put on your very own show!

By the way, 'break a leg' means 'good luck' in the world of the theatre. Theatre folk have lots of funny expressions, but don't worry, I'll explain them as we go along.

Let's start by finding out where we can put on a show ...

Macbeth by
William Shakespeare

All the World's a Stage

One of the exciting things about putting on a show is that you really can do it anywhere.

This quote is from a character in *A Midsummer Night's Dream*, one of Shakespeare's most famous and most performed plays. Peter Quince is a member of a penniless group of actors without a theatre to rehearse in, so he has decided to rehearse on a piece of grass or a 'plot'.

What image does the word 'theatre' conjure up in your head? You probably think of a large building with rows of seats and a stage with a curtain. Many theatres are like this, but not all of them. There are theatres in weird and wonderful places and theatres in lots of shapes and sizes.

Regent's Park in London is well known for its zoo, but it is also famous for having a theatre. There are no walls because it's outdoors and is known as an open-air theatre.

Does that sound like a good idea? What might be problematic?

The weather! Even though the theatre is only open between May and September each year, the audience are warned to bring warm clothes and umbrellas. The people who run the theatre say that the risk of rain and a bit of cold is what makes the theatre more like the original theatres from hundreds of years ago, most of which were outdoors.

The Bregenz Festival in Austria has a unique **venue** for musical and opera performances: a floating stage! Every summer, thousands of people sit on the shores of Lake Constance to watch shows on the spectacular stage. The directors of the James Bond film *Quantam of Solace* were so impressed with the setting, they filmed some scenes there during a production of an opera called *Tosca*.

Production of Verdi's opera *A Masked Ball*

The Minack Theatre in Cornwall is an open-air theatre on the very edge of England! It has a large, curved seating area so that the audience is almost on three sides of the stage. This shape resembles the theatres in Roman and Greek times.

DID YOU KNOW?

It is still possible, by law, for police to remove theatre goers in Winnetka, Illinois for having smelly feet!

There are many theatres today where the audience sit on all four sides. This is called theatre-in-the-round. The threesixty° Theatre Company performs in-the-round in an outdoor tent. Theatre-in-the-round makes the job of acting more difficult. The actors have to constantly make sure that all sides of the audience are involved in the action and that they aren't seeing too much of the actors' backs!

Street theatre is literally performed in the street, or maybe in a park or shopping centre – in fact, anywhere an audience will gather and watch. Street theatre might involve a play or some kind of specialist theatrical skill such as mime, fire-eating, juggling or singing and dancing. The actors often travel around, performing in different venues.

One of the most famous collections of street theatre is the Edinburgh Festival Fringe in Scotland, which takes place every year in the summer. Edinburgh comes alive with theatre all over the city, and performances are often on the streets. Shows have taken place in some surprising venues, including a public toilet, a fudge shop, someone's flat, a mystery island 20 kilometres off the Scottish coast and a swimming pool!

Some theatres are very small. One of the smallest theatres is in an old toilet! Named The Theatre of Small Convenience, it was bought from the local council and renovated by Dennis Neale, who now runs it as a non-profit business, which is a good thing because it only seats twelve people!

It is a puppet theatre and Dennis does five-minute shows. There is no booking – you just turn up between 2 pm and 5 pm and ask for a show. Dennis says, "It's almost like street theatre, but off the street."

Being in a small theatre can have its advantages. Because the audience are very close to the performers, it can make them feel that they are directly involved in the action – they can see the tiniest of movements on the faces of the actors. These small theatres are often called 'black box' theatres.

The Royal Albert Hall

DID YOU KNOW?

The record for the highest performance of a play was broken on the 23rd of April 2014 on an easyJet flight with a performance of Shakespeare's *The Gentlemen of Verona* at 37 000 feet.

Some theatres are enormous! The Hammersmith Apollo and the Royal Albert Hall in London have space for over 5000 people. There are so many different types of seats that they all have different names – and prices! Usually, the closer you are to the action, the more expensive your ticket.

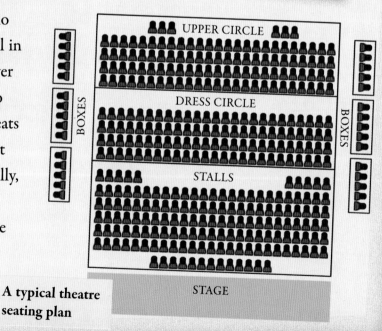

A typical theatre seating plan

UPPER CIRCLE

DRESS CIRCLE

STALLS

BOXES

BOXES

STAGE

DO IT YOURSELF!

If you wanted to put on a play or show, where would you do it? You'd need to think about two things. First of all, is there enough space for the actors to perform? Secondly, is there enough room for the audience and can they see the action easily? You could use your school hall, or do you have a community centre or a local hall you could use? In the summer why not use the park? If all else fails, put on a play in your own back garden or even your bedroom!

What a purr-formance!

Believe it or not, cats have a long tradition of working in the theatre. Historically, they earned their keep by catching mice, but often they were just company for the actors.

AMBROSE
lived at the
Drury Lane Theatre
in LONDON.
He enjoyed making appearances on stage – much to the annoyance of famous actor
Michael Crawford
who complained about being upstaged by a cat!

Boy Cat and Girl Cat
lived at the
Noel Coward
Theatre in London.
Boy Cat once disgraced himself by eating
PRINCESS
Margaret's bouquet
during a
Royal Gala performance.

There is one theatre where cats are actually the performers! At the Moscow Cat Theatre there are over 100 cats which are trained to perform all kinds of tricks.

What Kind of Show?

So, what kind of show do you want to put on? Do you want to make people laugh or cry or gasp with amazement? Do you want to make people think about important issues? Is the show for children, for adults or for both?

Musicals

Musicals are great shows because they are a mixture of acting, singing and dancing. They can make us laugh and cry because music can **provoke** very strong emotions. A musical can be hard work to produce, though.

The Lion King is a very complicated musical to stage. The actors have to be trained to sing and dance in huge headdresses – the tallest ones are 5.5 metres high – and some of the animal costumes are controlled electronically. There are 700 costumes to deal with and the director has to co-ordinate a **cast** of 52, with 113 in the backstage crew.

When another famous musical, *The Phantom of the Opera*, goes on tour to other theatres, it takes 27 lorries to transfer the set.

DID YOU KNOW?

The Lion King is based on the plot of Shakespeare's *Hamlet*.

Drama

The word 'drama' describes plays that usually have a serious theme. A drama might be a thriller or a story about tensions between people. The aim of a good drama is to create an emotional connection between the audience and the characters.

War Horse, based on the novel by Michael Morpurgo, is a good example of how drama draws the audience in. This theatre production transports the audience into the horror of World War I, as its hero Albert Narracott joins the army to search for his beloved horse, Joey.

DID YOU KNOW?

The longest running musical in the world is *Les Misérables*. Translated into over 20 languages, it has been running since 1985. There have been over 40 000 professional performances all around the world and it has won over 100 international awards.

Comedy

If you are putting on a comedy you need actors who are good at making people laugh. Some actors specialize in comedy and become very skilled at entertaining people, not only through their actions, but also the way they deliver their lines.

Some comedies are called farces. The plots in farces are usually exaggerated to the point of being ridiculous, and they include a lot of physical humour, like someone walking in a funny, over-the-top manner. Other comedies, called satires, highlight political or social issues in an amusing way.

DO IT YOURSELF!

When you're considering what kind of show to put on, you need to think about what you're good at. Are you a great singer? Then put on a musical. Are you the class clown? Comedy is the thing for you. Are you a confident actor? Classics or drama could be the way to go.

Don't forget to think about what your audience would enjoy too!

DID YOU KNOW?

Elizabethan theatres used coloured flags to advertise the type of play that would be performed that day. Red for history, white for comedy and black for tragedy.

Classics

Isn't it amazing that plays written hundreds of years ago are still being performed in theatres today? It makes you wonder if the playwrights who wrote them ever thought their plays would last so long!

Actors have to be specially trained to deliver the old English dialogue. Many of these older plays are Restoration comedies, which were written after Charles II was restored to the throne in 1660. A good way of telling if you are watching a Restoration comedy is if the characters have names that suggest something about them, such as Sir Courtly Nice, Mrs Dainty Fidget or Sir Davy Dunce.

DID YOU KNOW?

In Georgian times, theatres had wooden panels called kicking boards. The audience would kick them if they were getting bored. But the Ancient Greeks stamped their feet to show they were enjoying a play!

Restoration play *The Beaux' Stratagem* by George Farquhar

Behind the Scenes

In a fashion show, when flawless models appear on the catwalk, there are teams of people who have checked their hair and clothes and even helped them to rehearse how they should walk. The same is true of a theatre production; a lot of the success of the show is down to a team of professionals who work behind the scenes. These professionals **interpret** the script, visualize the staging, adapt and rehearse the play and organize the cast and crew.

BACKSTAGE CREW

TECHNICAL TEAM

WARDROBE

STAGE MANAGER

DIRECTOR

The producer

Hello there. I'm the producer. Basically, I'm the boss! That's because I manage the money. I have to find sponsors to financially support the production before it gets to the stage.

Without sponsorship we'd never be able to put on a show, so I have lots of connections in the business world. Sometimes I have to find huge sums of money. It can cost between 10 and 15 million dollars to open a big musical in New York's theatre district, Broadway.

I also arrange the venue for the production and hire the cast and crew, including key people such as the director.

Shrek the Musical cost 25 million dollars to make!

The director

Hello! I'm the director. I'm responsible for the creative side of a show. I **liaise** with lots of people involved in the play.

First of all, I have to be careful to stay within the budget given to me by the producer. I also work with the actors, singers and dancers, as well as those responsible for costumes, make-up, lighting, sound and set design to make sure we're all working towards the same artistic goal.

I arrange the timetable for the rehearsals and then lead them, giving the actors notes on how they can interpret the play. It has to make a connection with them because we want the audience to enjoy the play and recommend it to their friends and family.

The playwright usually has strong ideas about the characters in his or her play. I have to understand this so I can explain it to the actors, who can then pass it on to the audience. Sometimes I come up with my own interpretation, often in discussion with the actors.

With Shakespeare plays or other old scripts, directors have to decide a few things for themselves – there's no chance of asking the playwright!

The stage manager

Hi! I'm the stage manager and my job is the busiest of all! I'm the link between the cast and the production team. I have to:

- ☑ **delegate** jobs to members of the backstage crew
- ☑ record the positions of all the characters on stage
- ☑ write down all the lighting, sound and set changes and communicate them to the team
- ☑ record how many hours the actors rehearse
- ☑ check that everyone is there on performance days and that all equipment is working correctly
- ☑ take over from the director when the play is ready to perform
- ☑ make sure that all the costumes and props are returned and that the set is taken down properly

The musical director

Hello. I'm the musical director. I'm responsible for all the musical aspects of the play and for interpreting the music in the same way the director interprets the script. What is said and what is done on the stage is so closely linked to the music that the director and I must agree on how it will be performed.

Profile

Andrew Lloyd Webber is a very famous British composer and musical director who has written some of the most successful musicals ever, such as *Cats* and *The Phantom of the Opera*.

CATS

The choreographer

Hi! I'm the choreographer! I create the dance routines and teach them to the performers. I study three things very carefully before deciding on the dancers' moves. First I study the script (the words of the play), then the *libretto* (the script plus the words of the songs) and lastly, the score (the actual music).

Then I train the dancers. The dance moves are written in a special language called choreographic notation. Sometimes choreographers even create fight sequences and teach actors how to perform them safely, but more about that later!

Starting Off

Obviously without the actors, no production would ever happen. But how do you actually start acting? Most people who are interested in drama start acting at school, like I did. If you don't feel confident enough to act straight away, start small. Could you be the narrator in a school play, for example? Once you get a little experience of being in front of an audience, you'll feel more confident on stage. Or you could try to get some behind-the-scenes experience.

Me in a production of *As You Like It*, 1982

Youth theatre

Lots of towns have youth theatres or drama groups that you can join. The Pegasus Theatre in Oxford houses the Oxford Youth Theatre. It specializes in teaching a range of performing arts to young people and is supported by children's author Philip Pullman. Children can attend classes every week, after school and at the weekends, and work towards putting on a show at the end of each term. Students learn about all aspects of stagecraft. They don't have to perform if they don't want to, and can work on costumes or stage management instead.

Stage school and university

Some children go one step further and attend a special stage school, rather than a regular school. These schools often have links with film and theatre agents, so children can gain professional experience in film, television and theatre whilst still at school.

The majority of actors attend a normal school, just like I did, and then go on to study drama at college or university.

Emma Watson

FACTFILE

STARTED ACTING: Age 6

WHERE: School and youth theatre

MOST FAMOUS ROLE: Hermione Granger in the *Harry Potter* series

Zac Efron

FACTFILE

STARTED ACTING: Age 11

WHERE: School

MOST FAMOUS ROLE: Troy Bolton in *High School Musical*

Daniel Craig

FACTFILE

STARTED ACTING: Age 6

WHERE: School and the National Youth Theatre

MOST FAMOUS ROLE: James Bond

Acting is a tricky career. Many actors are often unemployed. It's important to have a good education so that you can do other jobs when there isn't any acting work.

Auditioning

Whether you want a part in a school play or a **West End** production, you'll probably need to audition. You will have to prepare an audition piece if you are an actor, a personal routine if you are a dancer, or a song (about one minute long) if you are trying for a singing role. If you are auditioning for a musical, you will be expected to do all three! The wider your skills, the wider your choice of what you can audition for.

The audition can be a nerve-wracking process and competition is fierce.

There are several different kinds of auditions:
- In 'monologue' auditions, you read, sing or dance a prepared piece on your own.
  - In a 'cold read' audition, you are asked to read the play as a group, and are given different parts to read in different scenes.
  - In an 'improvisation exercise', you are asked to perform scenes which you haven't prepared for.

So, what might impress the director? What kinds of things are they thinking about during the audition?

We're doing a historical play, but they've chosen an extract from a modern play ... Was that a good idea?

Is the actor actually performing, or just reciting the lines with no emotion?

How well does this person work with the others?

Is this audition interesting and is the actor making me feel any emotion?

Do they really understand the script?

Does the actor understand the character?

Rehearsing

In any production, the aim of the cast and crew is to be perfect for the opening night, so the rehearsal process, from early run-throughs to the dress rehearsal, is a serious business.

For a professional production, actors may rehearse for anything up to six or seven weeks. Rehearsals allow the actors to understand the play better and better as time goes on. They constantly develop their ability to interpret the playwright's words so they can create a connection with the audience.

Reading the script

The first rehearsal is a read-through. This is exactly what it sounds like: the actors sit around a table with their copies of the script and read through the play together from start to finish. This allows the director to explain different points as they work through the play.

Rehearsals

Next comes the period of rehearsals, when the actors really get to know the play and become comfortable with their lines. They also need to learn all their movements and their **cues**, which includes learning when to enter and exit the stage – not forgetting which side!

Tech week

The final week of rehearsals is called technical week, or 'tech week' for short. Before this, the actors may have been rehearsing in a different place, but during tech week, they rehearse in the venue itself, with all the technical elements of the production in place. These include:

- costumes
- make-up
- sets
- lighting
- sound.

By the start of tech week, the actors need to have learnt their lines and be completely comfortable with the director's interpretation of the play.

The purpose of tech week is to iron out any physical problems with the production. For example, an actor may discover that their costume is restrictive and that they can't move easily in a fight sequence.

Tech week is a very hectic time and can be stressful because everyone is trying to fix problems in the run-up to opening night.

Dress rehearsal

DID YOU KNOW?

There is a superstition amongst actors that a bad dress rehearsal will mean a good opening night.

The final rehearsal is called the dress rehearsal. This is treated as a real performance. There may sometimes be a very small audience for a dress rehearsal.

Put on a show!

Stage combat

One thing that needs a lot of rehearsing is stage combat. This creates the illusion of characters fighting on stage. It began in medieval theatre and became very common in Elizabethan theatre. Many of Shakespeare's most famous plays, like *Hamlet* or *Romeo and Juliet*, have fight scenes.

Stage combat can be physical combat between actors, or it can involve a variety of weapons.

The safety of the actors is critical. If a fight sequence is not properly choreographed, actors can be injured. Fight choreographers work hard to make sure this doesn't happen. Most are skilled in several types of fighting, such as martial arts. They'll usually be experienced in sword fighting too, which is useful for classic plays where a lot of stage combat involves swords.

Fencing moves are adapted for the stage to make sure that the tip of the sword does not come near the face of another actor; attacking actions are always aimed to just miss the opponent. All stage violence, even smaller actions like slapping a face or twisting an arm, is done so that the audience thinks they have seen something they have not. It is up to the actor playing the victim to make it appear that they have been hurt. They do this by using their facial and bodily actions, and also some sound effects.

A fight choreographer may sketch out the sequence of movements for each actor. They'll also ensure that the stage area is completely safe, by checking that the lighting doesn't block an actor's view, or that props or furniture won't get damaged during the fight. Performers practise the routine, slowly at first, until they are confident enough to do it at a pace is that is convincing but safe.

Before every performance there is a rehearsal called a 'fight call', which is for actors to run through the fight. They do this to increase their ability to perform the movements automatically. This is called 'muscle memory'.

The actors need to perform the fight scene automatically because they need to stay in character while doing it. No matter how good the fight choreography, it won't move the action along, or tell us anything about the characters, unless the actors can play their roles convincingly at the same time.

DID YOU KNOW?

Fight choreographers call the sound of actors hitting each other a 'knap'.

What to Wear and What to Use

If you are putting on a show, you want the audience to believe in the characters, to feel that the person on the stage really is a penniless artist, a businesswoman, a pirate or a duchess. Costumes and make-up help the audience to believe in the characters.

Costumes

A good costume gives the audience information about the character as soon as they appear on the stage. For instance, if a character is rich, this will show in the type of clothes they wear. If, however, the character is a penniless orphan, this will be clear immediately through their ragged clothes. The audience should be able to tell which **era** the play is set in and where in the world it is.

Costumes really help actors to get into character. One of the best ways to *feel* like a medieval peasant is to *dress* like one!

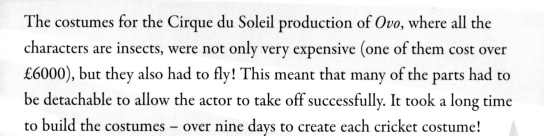

A cricket from *Ovo*, Cirque du Soleil

The costumes for the Cirque du Soleil production of *Ovo*, where all the characters are insects, were not only very expensive (one of them cost over £6000), but they also had to fly! This meant that many of the parts had to be detachable to allow the actor to take off successfully. It took a long time to build the costumes – over nine days to create each cricket costume!

DID YOU KNOW?

The Disney World Theatre has the biggest collection of costumes in the world – there are 1.2 million!

"Insect comes from the Latin word 'insecta' that means 'in section'. So all the costumes are sectioned with many parts, like our bodies with our muscles."

Liz Vandal, Costume Designer, *Ovo*

The costume designer's vision is made real by a team of buyers and tailors. The team have to think carefully not only about the budget, but also about the effect of lights on the costumes and how they fit in with the set design.

The costume department of a large theatre has to be experienced in dyeing, printing, leatherwork, beading, mask-making and jewellery design, among other skills.

Some types of theatre, like Japanese Noh theatre, have very extravagant costumes. Masks are only worn by the main character. They are far more important than props as they show a character's personality. There are five different types of masks: gods, demons, men, women and the elderly.

DID YOU KNOW?

Many costume designers now avoid zips and velcro – they cannot risk a zip getting caught during a quick costume change and velcro is just too noisy! They often use industrial strength magnets to fasten the clothes.

DO IT YOURSELF!

When you're putting on a show, you'll need to find some costumes. You probably don't have a huge budget, so you'll need to be inventive! Start close to home – you may have a dressing-up box that you can look in. Perhaps some family members have some old clothes they want to get rid of? Remember to ask them first!

If you can't find anything at home, you may be able to buy items for your costumes at charity shops, jumble sales or car boot sales. It's amazing what you can find. I once found a genuine cowboy hat at a car boot sale. It came in pretty handy!

Make-up

State-of-the-art theatre lighting can transform an actor's face so much that they only need to wear natural make-up or none at all. However, a lot of actors are required to transform their appearance, so the make-up department still has plenty of work to do. Certain features can be either highlighted or reduced. In this way a face can, for example, be made to look thin or old.

Becoming older

STEP 1

STEP 2

STEP 3

Becoming the Phantom of the Opera

STEP 1

STEP 2

STEP 3

STEP 4

STEP 5

STEP 6

Skilled make-up artists can achieve even more amazing transformations through the use of **prosthetics**. They can make an actor unrecognizable. Two different types of **rubber** that are often used to make masks are silicone and latex. Starting with a mould of the actor's face and adding parts made from these materials, a make-up artist can create double chins, scars, huge noses, horns, battle wounds, boils and many other unusual facial features.

Becoming Shrek

Of course, you'll need to do your own make-up for your show. You won't have a make-up artist to help you. So how can you get started? You can buy face paints very easily in toy shops or fancy dress shops.

STEP 1

STEP 2

STEP 3

STEP 4

STEP 5

STEP 6

DID YOU KNOW?

At one point in Shakespeare's *King Lear*, one of the characters' eyes pop out! In a recent production, plums covered in fake blood were used to make realistic eyeballs.

How to make fake blood

One of the jobs of the make-up team is to produce **artificial** blood when required. Here's how you can do it for your own show!

You will need:

- Cornflour
- Water
- Blue or green food colouring
- Golden syrup
- Red food colouring

1 Mix one tablespoon of cornflour with a cup of golden syrup. Don't worry if the mixture is really thick and gloopy – it's supposed to be like that!

2 Once the two ingredients are mixed, start to add a bit of water at a time. Keep going until it's a similar thickness to blood. You'll probably need between ¼ and ½ cup.

3 You should now have a pale substance which looks nothing like blood. So it's time to add the red food colouring. It's quite strong so only add a few drops at a time, making sure you mix it in after each addition.

4 Now to add the finishing touches! Real blood isn't bright red, but you can change the effect by using a few drops of blue or green food colouring.

5 Your fake blood should be looking pretty convincing by now. Even if you can't wait to use it, leave it alone for a few minutes to allow it to thicken.

WARNING: This fake blood will stain your clothes and your skin. Don't make it the day before your school photograph!

Props

Anything that is on the stage, and not part of the set or a costume, is called a prop, which is short for property. This includes the furniture, weapons and anything that an actor brings onto the stage, whether it is a cat or a pen.

The use of props increased in Elizabethan theatre. This was because the first permanent theatres were built during this period. Before that, travelling troupes (groups) of players had performed plays in public spaces. They had to carry everything they needed with them, so they didn't use many props.

In large theatres, there is a team of prop makers who usually work for a set designer. The team is skilled in carpentry, sculpture, weaving, moulding, furniture-making, metalwork and model-making. They have to do a lot of research in order to make the props look as **authentic** as possible. This is an important part of ensuring the audience have a good experience – they need to believe that the situation is real.

DID YOU KNOW?

The most expensive prop ever was the car in *Chitty Chitty Bang Bang* which cost £750 000 to make – but, then, it does fly!

Some props can be hazardous. Actors have been injured when retractable blades failed to retract! Being stabbed isn't part of an actor's job description, so nowadays these types of blades are not recommended. Weapons are usually hired from companies that specialize in making theatrical weapons, due to the highly skilled work needed to make them look (and sound) right.

DID YOU KNOW?

When he died in 1982, a Polish pianist called André Tchaikowsky donated his skull to the Royal Shakespeare Company to be used as a prop. For many years no one thought they should use it in plays. The first actor to do so was former Dr Who, David Tennant, while playing Hamlet.

What You Hear and What You See

In the theatre, lighting can create different moods. It is also used to carry out several different jobs.

Focus attention

A director can use light to focus all the attention on the action that is happening on one part of the stage only. Alternatively, the director may use lighting to distract the audience from something that is happening on another part of the stage, like some scenery being changed.

Establish the time of day

Blue light suggests night and orange and red light can represent a sunset. Colours are created through filters placed in the lamps. Shapes are created using 'gobos', which are cutouts that are slotted into the lamps. The resulting shape (the moon, for example) can be projected onto the back of the stage.

The effects of stage lighting

Change appearances

Try shining a torch under your face and looking in the mirror. Pretty scary, eh? Another way to make yourself look creepy is to use blue light, which washes out colour and will make you look very pale.

In a scene in *Macbeth*, where Macbeth has just killed the king, the director may choose to light the actor from above. This creates bags under the eyes and the chin and makes him look tired or ill.

In a musical like *Cats*, angled front lighting is often used to highlight all the features of the **elaborate** make-up – whiskers and all.

DID YOU KNOW?

Stage technicians never refer to 'bulbs'. They are always called 'lamps'.

Create scenery

Costume, make-up and set designers work closely together to test the effect of lighting on everything that is going to appear on the stage. Red light will turn green scenery grey, so if you have a background of grass or trees, a solution has to be found if you want the green colour to stay green!

In the Broadway production of *The Wizard of Oz*, many light projections were used to create scenery, including background images of tornadoes.

Cats by Andrew
Lloyd Webber

Lighting changes according to:

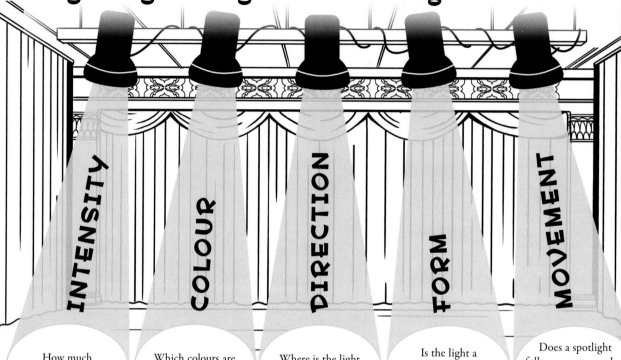

INTENSITY
How much light is there?

COLOUR
Which colours are used to create effect?

DIRECTION
Where is the light coming from?

FORM
Is the light a thin beam or a broad beam?

MOVEMENT
Does a spotlight follow an actor as they move, or stay fixed on one point?

A great example of staging and lighting working together is the 'scrim'. This is a very thin curtain which appears **opaque** if lit from the front or **transparent** if lit from behind.

DID YOU KNOW?

The first theatre in the UK was called ... The Theatre!

DO IT YOURSELF!

To create a spotlight, shine a torch on your actor. For backlighting, shine a small lamp through a thin scarf. Always ask an adult for help when managing your stage lighting and remember that bulbs can get very hot!

Sound

Sound production in the theatre is split into two main categories: **amplification** (the use of microphones) and sound effects (additional sounds to make the show seem more real, like the noise of gunfire to show a battle).

There are some people who think that actors should use their own vocal skills to make themselves heard clearly – after all, that was the way it was done for centuries. However, nowadays most actors wear body microphones, or 'shotgun' microphones are placed around the stage to pick up actors' voices.

Today, most sound effects are produced digitally, which means that the range of sounds is almost limitless! Sound effects that are produced by the actions of characters, for example general chatter in the background of a busy street, are called motivated sounds. Sound effects that recreate natural sounds, like running water or birdsong, are known as environmental sounds.

A show that requires music will sometimes have its own orchestra. The musicians usually play in a lowered area at the front of the stage called the pit.

DO IT YOURSELF!

Do you need music for your show? You don't need an orchestra – just use an MP3 player with a portable mini speaker. Remember to choose your soundtrack carefully. Music has a really important effect on the emotions of the audience. It can make them cry or jump with fright! Make sure your music isn't too loud – you don't want it to drown out the voices of the actors.

Set design

The set is the decoration on the stage which gives it a sense of place. The set designer discusses with the director exactly what they want the stage to look like. When the curtain opens, the set should create pictures and feelings to draw the audience in to the pretend world of the play.

Sometimes the design might be minimal, or very simple. This may be because the director and set designer want the audience to concentrate on the words of the play and not be distracted by elaborate scenery. Other set designs, like those for big London and New York musicals, can be very complicated and cost thousands of pounds.

The Lord of the Rings, 2007, was one of the most expensive productions ever staged.

The curtains at the front of the stage are called the house curtains and these are opened to reveal the stage. There is often another curtain at the back of the stage with scenery painted on it – this is a backdrop. Other things that make up a set are the flats, painted boards which are positioned all around the stage and look like buildings, trees or other backgrounds. Often platforms are used to create different levels on the stage.

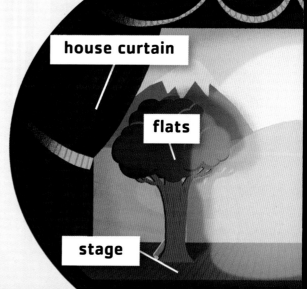

house curtain

flats

stage

In *The Phantom of the Opera*, a chandelier comprising 6000 beads swoops over the heads of the audience, a boat floats across the stage and a woman walks through a mirror – or appears to!

With the advance of technology and the use of computer-generated images, robotics and devices that allow walls and floors to rise and fall, set designers now have the ability to produce amazing effects. Sets can transform in front of our eyes and scenery can be projected by lasers so that real objects mix with **virtual** ones.

backdrop

audience

DO IT YOURSELF!

To create your own set it's great if you can use small items of furniture, such as chairs or stools. Make sure they are light enough to quickly lift off stage if you need to change the set. Why not paint a backdrop on an old sheet you can hang up at the back of the stage to really set the scene?

From Idea to Production

1 The play is chosen and the director and producer are found. If there are no 'resident' designers already at the theatre, the director decides on the designers. Auditions are held and the play is cast.

2 The director and various designers (set, costumes, make-up and technical) discuss the play and how they will interpret it. They may adapt these ideas during the rehearsals.

3 A choreographer may work with the actors to perfect the dance moves and a voice coach may be employed to help with accents.

4 Later in the rehearsal period, the technical staff begin to set up the lighting and the set is built. During tech week, they rehearse lighting and sound cues with the actors.

5 The musical director and assistants (like singing coaches) rehearse the singing with the performers.

6 Those responsible for costumes and props work on their specific areas. Later the costumes are tried on and the props are tried out. Then make-up ideas are tested.

7 The publicity team decide how and where to advertise in order to get as many people as possible to come and see the play.

8 Before the performance launches, a dress rehearsal takes place to make sure that every element works as it should do.

9 The 'front of house' team makes sure that everything runs smoothly for the audience.

10 On the day of the performance, the backstage crew are on hand to move scenery. The stage manager makes sure everything is running as it should behind the scenes.

By now you'll have seen that putting a show takes a lot of work, but once the audie is applauding, all the effort will have been wort

Putting on a show means that a lot of people all w towards a common goal – whether they are on the s or behind the scenes. Either way, it's a lot of fun! remember, you don't actually need a theatre because you put on a show anywhere. All you really need is enthus and imagination. Good luck! I mean, break a

Glossary

amplification: making something louder

artificial: not real

authentic: real, genuine

cast: group of performers

cues: signals which tell you when something should happen

delegate: give someone else a job to do

elaborate: having lots of detail

era: time period

interpret: develop your own understanding of something

liaise: communicate with different people or groups

opaque: solid, cannot be seen through

prosthetics: materials that are added to a performer's face to change their appearance

provoke: create a feeling or response

rubber: springy, elastic material

state-of-the-art: the newest and most modern features

transparent: clear, can be seen through

venue: location where events take place

virtual: computer-generated

West End: London's theatre district

Index

About the Author

I have lived in Morocco for quite a few years and before that in Turkey, Sudan, Egypt and Saudi Arabia. I suppose I like hot places! At the moment I live in an old pirate city called Salé in a tiny flat with a very big cat.

I have been a teacher for a long time and now I teach teachers how to use theatrical techniques in their classrooms. I have directed many school plays and hope I will direct many more.

A really good piece of theatre has a lot of work behind it. I have always loved the theatre because it is a bit more dangerous than making films or most television programmes. Things can go wrong because it's live!

Greg Foot, Series Editor

I've loved science ever since the day I took my papier mâché volcano into school. I filled it with far too much baking powder, vinegar and red food colouring, and WHOOSH! I covered the classroom ceiling in red goo. Now I've got the best job in the world: I present TV shows for the BBC, answer kids' science questions on YouTube, and make huge explosions on stage at festivals!

Working on TreeTops inFact has been great fun. There are so many brilliant books, and guess what ... they're all packed full of awesome facts! What's your favourite?